SOUTHERN WAY

Spec

C000181833

SOUTHERN COLOUR IN THE SIXTIES

a personal selection

Terry Cole

NOODLE BOOKS

© Kevin Robertson (Noodle Books) and Terry Cole 2008

ISBN   978-1-9554110-9-0

First published in 2008 by Kevin Robertson
under the **NOODLE BOOKS** imprint
PO Box 279
Corhampton
SOUTHAMPTON
SO32 3ZX

www.kevinrobertsonbooks.co.uk

Printed in England by the Alden Press

Front cover - The Hayling Island Line, Summer 1963. A1X class 32650 runs over Langston crossing on its way to Hayling Island. The crossing gates were manually operated and with a train every 15 minutes at peak times both a signalman and a crossing keeper were required. In the waiting queue of traffic are a red Mini and a 250cc Royal Enfield Crusader Sports motorcycle.

Frontispiece - 'Waving to the train': an almost universal reaction to a passing train in the days of steam. Here, at one of my favourite locations on the Hayling Island line, just north of Langston, a group of children ran to the occupation crossing to wave just as I was taking the picture. The simple pleasures of sixties childhood.

Opposite - The Ryde to Ventnor line on the Isle of Wight. An Adams O2 class 0-4-4T climbs Apse bank between Shanklin and Wroxall in summer 1965. Culver Cliffs can be seen in the distance. The sturdy little Adams engines had no difficulty in hauling 6 coaches up this steep climb.

Back cover - Autumn 1963. An A1X 'Terrier' class locomotive is almost lost to view as it heads its 2 coach train along the shore of Langstone Harbour towards the bridge across to Hayling Island..

(All photographs by the author.)

PREFACE

So what criteria determined this personal selection? Essentially a wish to present locomotives, carriages and wagons in operation at a specific moment in time. The final choice depended on the whim of the photographer and was governed by the distance he was able to travel by bike, train or car on any one day out.

To fill in some detail, my interest in Railways began at an early age but in 1954, when I was 10, we moved to West Worthing to a house right next to the railway line and this really set me off. A newly acquired ABC spotters' book now made it possible to identify the steam engines I was seeing everyday and shortly afterwards I started taking photos of them with my 'Brownie 127'. The aim was of course to picture them in their settings like a 'proper' railway photographer did, but my camera, with its slow shutter speed, wasn't up to the job. Eventually however I saved enough to buy an antique 35mm camera, which did give a slightly faster shutter speed when the light was good! Photographs had to be in black and white because colour film was quite beyond the reach of weekly pocket money. Towards the end of the 1950s I did take some cine film on the grounds that if I was going to save up for colour I might as well have moving colour! But it wasn't until 1963 that I started taking slides. What a revelation! Being able to see the images projected onto a screen with all the vibrant detail was to be my goal from now on. The bright colours were captivating and the intensity of the light could be used to spectacular effect. Here were my beloved steam trains captured in all their glory in beautiful countryside.

However, the eleventh hour was at hand. Most of the steam engines of my childhood had already gone and the rest were disappearing fast. This called for urgent action moving from one line to the next trying to capture the scene before it was too late. Admittedly this race against time meant that much was neglected on my doorstep. Hindsight is, as ever, a wonderful thing. Nonetheless, as this publication illustrates, I did manage to capture many favourite scenes before steam was swept away and the lines closed down for good.

The photographs included are grouped into chapters each of which covers a particular line. In this way I have tried to recreate my days spent train spotting rather than attempting an all embracing picture of the region. My hope is that this in depth look at individual lines will be of interest to those who wish to indulge in pure nostalgia as well as to modellers and railway historians.

Thanks are due to members of the Sussex Area HMRS who have offered suggestions and additional information which has been incorporated into this book.

I hope you, the readers, will share the enjoyment that I experienced in compiling this selection and that it will convey something of the lost beauty of our steam railways.

Terry Cole

Steyning, April 2008

CONTENTS

Introduction

After the Second World War the Railways of this country were inevitably very run down. Locomotives and Rolling Stock alike were in poor shape having been heavily used with minimal maintenance. Little replacement had been authorised with the result that the fleet was ageing, not to mention the considerable losses incurred through war damage. A sorry picture emerges. Post-war the Big Four Companies (LMS, LNER, GWR and SR) looked forward to better times but little money was available for improvement. The Southern Railway in particular had high hopes of substantially increasing its pre-war holiday traffic together with extensive plans for further electrification. However the newly elected Labour Government decided that a national asset as important as the Railways should not be allowed to continue in private ownership because these owners could not be depended on to have the will and the necessary capital to make the improvements it considered essential. Furthermore it concluded that there was good reason to establish a truly integrated national network. And so on 1st January 1948 the railways were nationalised. An ambitious modernisation programme began. The ultimate aim was to produce 'Standard' designs for locomotives and coaches but this could not be done overnight. Consequently construction continued for a while using the best of the 'old' companies' designs. Freight rolling stock was massively improved with tens of thousands of replacement wagons built to new specifications. All this was achieved despite chronic shortages of materials, many staple commodities still being rationed, and an economy which was being propped up only by American loans.

By the mid 1950s the situation had been transformed: most of the antiquated and worn out items of stock had been withdrawn and the railway system had acquired, or was rapidly acquiring, a modern and efficient fleet. Meanwhile the next 'modernisation plan' had already been devised. It was revolutionary and foresaw the end of steam working. Although its aim was the electrification of major routes it was recognised that this would be expensive both in terms of time and cost. So in the interim new diesel locomotives and multiple units were to be constructed and the building of steam locomotives was to cease after the end of the current programme. (The last steam locomotive, 'Evening Star', was in fact to be completed in 1960).

The Government had changed by the mid fifties. The need for such an extensive railway network was starting to be questioned especially as the railways continued to lose money. It was a fact that on occasions the Big Four companies themselves had withdrawn services on little used lines and this had continued through the early days of nationalisation without any fuss. For example the Lewes to East Grinstead line, featured in this book, was one of those closed without ceremony in May 1955 because it was uneconomic. However, up till this time, it was widely accepted that the railways were an essential component of the country's infrastructure.

Then something changed! The devastating National Rail Strike of spring 1955 proved to be a turning point for the industry. The Government suddenly realised that the country could be shut down by the railway unions! Their power must to be curtailed! This realisation and reaction were to be echoed in relation to the Miners' Strikes in the 1970s. So the government started encouraging the transfer of traffic from rail to road. The assumption that the Railways were essential had gone!

A national debate began as to whether the Railways should be run as a public service or primarily as a paying business. If a line did not earn its keep should it be retained with subsidies or should it be closed? It so happened that the latter was not necessarily a straightforward process: a freak event, of little importance in itself, was to have a profound effect. A local resident discovered that the closure of the Lewes and East Grinstead line was illegal, as the original Act of Parliament required the operation in perpetuity of a minimum service. British Railways were forced to reopen the line and run that service, which they did without much grace, whilst seeking a further Act of Parliament permitting closure. It was this line which as the Bluebell Railway was to herald the start of the standard gauge railway preservation movement. The national debate really kicked off now. Unfortunately for the advocates of the railways as a public service this was a very bad example on which to have to fight for their cause. The line, especially the south section, was hopelessly uneconomic and little used. The northern section, which the Southern Railway had intended to electrify before the war, was not really viable on its own. Not surprisingly the Act of Parliament was passed and line closed for a second time in the1958. Although in a general sense the public service argument rumbled on for a while, the case was all but lost.

The last steam locomotive entered service in 1960. Meanwhile a bewildering number of different types of diesel locomotive had been purchased or ordered. Construction of the latter was very much more expensive than their steam counterparts and some of the designs were unproven. In spite of these problems such was the headlong rush to stem the Railway's operating losses that considerable sums were spent on new diesels in order to save money. This they did. However some were to prove 'white elephants' and the multiplicity of designs did little for the desired standardisation or reduction of maintenance overheads. The Minister of Transport, Ernest Marples, had meanwhile been responsible for promoting the diversion of goods traffic to the roads starving the railways of much of their staple income. In his role as the part owner of a construction company which was busy building new roads and motorways he was hardly impartial. But this fact seems to have been ignored! At his request a plan to radically reduce the railway network was being developed by Dr Beeching. His initial report was too radical for even the Government, worried as it was by the effect it might have on marginal seats. The revised version, the notorious 'Beeching Report' of the early sixties proposed the radical pruning of a high proportion of branch lines together with those secondary and main lines which had been duplicated or those which were deemed economically unviable. About one third of the stations were to be closed along with a similar proportion of the route mileage. This was accepted by a government determined to 'cut until the railways made a profit': a panacea, as they saw it, for the ills of the nationalised railway. Implementation started straight away despite the fact that traffic had substantially increased on some of the lines as a result of improved services. Unfortunately there was a lack of understanding of the nature of railway travel and of the role of branch lines as essential feeders to mainlines. Because the cuts were implemented without a proper understanding of how the network functioned, losses continued.

However worse was to come. The road lobby was very much in the ascendancy especially now that the motorway building programme had begun. Did the railways have a future at all or were they now outdated? Should they be allowed to die like the canals

The Steyning line was a typical secondary route serving a collection of towns and villages. Here on a rather wet day in 1963 an unusually grimy BR Class 4 tank locomotive enters the down platform at West Grinstead with a train for Brighton.

that they had replaced? The first half of the sixties was very much a 'brave new world': at last the legacy of the war and its privations had been cast aside and the country could get on with living again. In all areas from architecture to popular culture the old was being discarded. 'New' meant better. As a consequence medieval buildings in historic market towns and even the iconic 'Doric Arch' at Euston were torn down to make way for sixties 'brutalism'. (St Pancras thankfully escaped, to be reborn in our present age, thanks to a campaign spearheaded by Sir John Betjeman). 'Modernisation' of the railways was getting into its stride, gaining a momentum all its own. The plan to eliminate steam traction was accelerating. Because the emphasis was on destruction accountants and planners no longer had to worry. Targets for reduction could be met on time or early with the mere stroke of a pen: another 500 locomotives to be condemned, another 20 lines proposed for closure. So it was that virtually all the remaining Southern steam locomotives built before 1923 were condemned en bloc on 31st December 1962, regardless of condition and even if they had been overhauled just a few months previously. This course of action constituted the squandering of national resources on a monumental scale and was not confined to the older locomotives. New locomotives with only a few years service were condemned for the most trivial of faults. It was not as if the country was prospering. Despite Harold Macmillan's famous 'you've never had it so good' the economic situation was pretty parlous. The full extent of this only became apparent when the Labour Government came to power in 1964. Britain was effectively bankrupt; overspending having produced a massive budget deficit. This would soon lead to a credit squeeze of even greater ferocity than our present 'credit crunch'. At the end of the decade the pound was devalued and the IMF called in to rescue the country from bankruptcy.

If the Conservative government had been very pro road then surely the incoming Labour administration with its pre election pledge to halt railway closures would revive the Railway's fortunes. It did not; in fact it was even worse. It proved to be even more 'anti rail' than its predecessor. Even though the extensive closure of lines under the Beeching plan reduced the overall mileage the widespread withdrawals of steam locomotives and coaches resulted in a drastic shortage of stock. British Rail wanted to buy more diesel multiple units to meet this shortfall but the government refused to sanction the funding. Hence further line closures had to be made. As the pressure to reduce losses increased some civil servants, who were anxious to smooth the passage for road improvement schemes, used dubious tactics to justify closures on 'economic grounds'. Even Beeching's recommendations were now being overtaken. The tap had been turned off and there was no money to buy new stock. Yet the elimination of steam was being forced through massively ahead of schedule and in a most draconian manner. It was complete madness. 'The railways are still losing money – close some more lines'. The Steyning line and the one from Eastbourne to Tunbridge Wells both suffered in this way as a result. Lines were officially classed as 'unremunerative', often on dubious grounds, so that when the Transport Users Consultative Committee duly met to consider the closure proposals, the outcome was predictable. Sentence was passed: 'closure agreed subject to the provision of additional bus services'. The latter, of course, would soon be deemed unnecessary. Even the important through route from Redhill to Reading would have closed had the 'Southern' not managed to cobble together some diesel multiple units from odd surplus items of stock. In the days of the Big Four and during the early years of British Railways every effort had been made to generate more traffic on ailing lines in order to avoid closures. Likewise in the early days of the modernisation programme, Diesel Multiple Units were introduced on many lines and travel was actively promoted often with dramatic improvements in passenger figures. However as the sixties progressed, this policy was replaced with a much harsher 'it pays or it goes' approach. In fact closures were often justified by the inclusion of all sorts of extraneous costs, whereas any positive impact, any real contribution to the network as a whole was ignored. Little consideration was paid to social need or indeed convenience and absolutely none to longer term transport requirements in the light of increased housing development and traffic congestion. The Railways were perceived to be outdated. It was felt that they had no place in Modern Britain. As a result the railway infrastructure was squandered. Indeed many of the lines which feature in this book would have been viable today, albeit with modifications, fulfilling a useful public service had they been retained. Were this the case we might not now be experiencing the present chronic vehicle emissions and congestion on our roads.

In conclusion popular culture often seems to have the knack of grasping a reality which is later recognised as an essential truth. Hence the enduring validity of the words sung by Joni Mitchell in the sixties song Big Yellow Taxi:

'….. you don't know what you've got till it's gone, they've paved paradise, put up a parking lot.'

Surely a telling comment on the nineteen-sixties.

CHAPTER 1

Trains in the Worthing Area

The times of the steam trains passing my West Worthing home, the comings and goings of the morning and evening freights which served the local yard, these were the familiar sights and sounds which punctuated my days. The old London Brighton and South Coast Railway ran west along the coast past our front door. By 1963 the Ks, E4s and C2X class engines, which for many years had worked the goods and van trains, had disappeared. One bright September morning it occurred to me that it was a matter of some urgency to capture what I could before it was too late.

What follows may appear to be a somewhat random series of shots but these do reflect the wide variety of steam workings in operation on just one section of a line which carried all manner of services. These ranged from long distance cross country passenger trains like the Brighton to Cardiff express, the local workers' train between Brighton and Lancing not forgetting the multiplicity of goods services whether reflecting the local economy of the area or part of the wider freight network.

Above - N class 31829 passes West Worthing electric train sheds, a short distance from my window. It has shunted a number of wagons from the goods yard behind the sheds and can be seen running round to collect them. This will be the return working of the morning freight to Worthing Central yard. The railway workers' allotments in the foreground show the good use made of spare land between the main lines and the fence.

Above - 31829 ambles along from West Worthing to Worthing Central having just passed the up advance starting signal for West Worthing. The station is just visible in the distance. On this occasion the load consists of just three wagons, which appear to be empty and a Southern Railway goods brake van. Only a couple of years earlier both the incoming and outgoing loads would have comprised 20 vehicles or more. On the down line a 4COR 'Nelson' electric unit is receding, probably working a semi fast to Portsmouth. These units, introduced for the London to Portsmouth service, gained the nickname Nelsons because of the asymmetric indicator blind on the end of the unit. This gave them a 'one eyed' appearance.

Opposite top - As 31829 heads towards Worthing Central we get a view over the tender. 31829 was one of the locomotives purchased by the Southern Railway in 1924 in 'part built' condition from Woolwich Arsenal. These had been constructed under a Government order to provide employment for the works after the First World War. They gave the Railway many years of excellent service and were always known as 'Woolworths', probably because they were bargain purchases. Locations for photography were limited in this area due to the proximity of houses and other obstructions.

Opposite lower - The same train has now run through Worthing Central station and reversed on to the down line in order to draw forward into the yard. The non electrified line on the right hand side of the picture served a two road loading platform for perishable traffic located at the far end of the station. The Worthing area had been a very important centre for tomato growing and other market garden produce. Van loads were dispatched every day. However by the 1960s the number of market gardens was rapidly declining as owners found it more profitable to sell land for housing development rather than to continue growing crops.

Opposite top - After the LBSCR Carriage Works moved from Brighton to Lancing in 1913 a train was run morning and evening for the workers. Known locally as the 'Lancing Belle' this train always featured somewhat antique rolling stock displaced from revenue earning traffic. Lancing was the main carriage works on the Southern dealing with the repair and overhaul of steam and electric stock and in the early 1960s this train still comprised 9 bogie coaches. With a seating capacity of over 700 this was some train! Each compartment had a number painted on the door presumably so that the workmen could easily find their usual seat. The train is seen here in October 1963 approaching Shoreham airport on its way back to Brighton. It comprises a selection of high capacity ex SECR and LSWR stock with an ex LSWR 'Ironclad' brake coach at the front and is hauled by two LMS designed class 2 41xxx locomotives.

Opposite lower - By June 1964 the works was being run down and the train, seen here leaving Lancing, is now reduced to 5 coaches hauled by diesel locomotive D6524. The Ironclad brake is still the leading vehicle but the middle vehicle is now S 1000 S, an experimental coach with a body built of fibreglass. This vehicle, known as 'the plastic coach' and easily identified by its white roof, saw service in a number of odd corners of the Southern system. Although successful it was destined to remain a one off.

Above - Here we see the same workers' train in the same location in May 1965 but this time hauled by a solitary Class 2 locomotive.

Opposite top - By 1963 freights along the coast line were pulled by Maunsell Q or N class locomotives. Unfortunately these trains often ran at night or at other times not conducive to good photography. Here a Q class locomotive on its way east with a freight train approaches Shoreham airport. The train has a brake van at each end so it may be destined for Brighton Top Yard which would require a reversal of direction at Preston Park. This locomotive is one of 6 fitted from 1958 onwards with a BR Standard Class 4 blast-pipe and single chimney in place of the Bulleid multiple jet blast-pipe and wide chimney. Despite the impending end of steam, modifications to improve engine performance continued to be made until the very last.

Opposite lower - BR Standard Class 4 tank 80014 is seen in June 1964 heading west past Shoreham airport with the daily Brighton to Cardiff train which it will haul as far as Salisbury. Rebuilt West Country Pacifics were more usual on this working because 80014 will need to replenish its water tanks en route. This was one of three cross country steam trains which ran daily along the west coast line. The site of the former Bungalow Town Halt, serving Shoreham Beach, which closed in 1933, is marked by the two concrete uprights in the left foreground. 80014 which was built at Brighton in September 1951 was the 5th member of this class to enter traffic. Initially allocated to Tunbridge Wells West for the London commuter services it moved to Brighton in September 1963. Its last days were spent at Eastleigh from where it was withdrawn in May 1965.

Above - Rebuilt West Country 34027 'Taw Valley' heads past Shoreham airport in 1963 with a Brighton – Plymouth train. This engine had been built at Brighton in April 1946 and rebuilt at Eastleigh in September 1957. 'Taw Valley' was withdrawn in August 1964 but survived in a scrap yard long enough to be bought for preservation and restored to working order.

The Steyning Line

This secondary route left the Brighton to Portsmouth mainline at Shoreham to head north along the banks of the River Adur, past the market town of Steyning, to eventually join the Mid Sussex line at Christ's Hospital just west of Horsham. Trains ran through from Brighton to Horsham although there was the odd working from Brighton which terminated at Steyning. The line was double track throughout and was often used as a relief line for the Brighton to London mainline and for through excursion workings. In the late 1950s trains were usually 2 or 3 coach push pull affairs hauled by an ex LSWR M7 tank engine based at either Horsham or Brighton. However by 1963 these had all gone and BR or ex LMS 'standard' designs had taken over.

Above - Shortly after leaving Shoreham the line passed Beeding Cement Works where there was an extensive sidings complex. A considerable volume of traffic originated here as shown by the length of the bulk cement train seen at the start of its journey from Beeding down to Shoreham behind N Class 2-6-0 No 31830 on a late summer evening in 1963.

Opposite top - The first passenger station on the line was Bramber. Its proximity to Steyning meant that it alone of the stations on the line did not have a goods yard. Summer 1963 and 41287, an LMS designed Class 2 locomotive, hauling a Bulleid 3 coach set bound for Horsham, enters Bramber station and passes the distant signal for Steyning. The locomotive, built at Crewe in November 1950 and transferred to the Southern Region in the early 1960s, was at this time based at Brighton.

Opposite lower - On the same day another Class 2 locomotive No 41325 leaves Bramber with a down train again formed of a Bulleid 3-coach set. Although to a design by LMS Chief Mechanical Engineer H G Ivatt, 30 of them (Nos. 41290 – 41319) were built after nationalisation specifically for use on the Southern Region where they replaced many older designs. These powerful locomotives with their comfortable cabs and easy preparation and disposal routines must have been welcome to the Brighton men used to the rather more rudimentary E4 or M7 tanks.

Opposite top - Bramber station building was on the up side of the line; a footbridge connected it to the down platform with its lengthy canopy. The entrance to the station was through the 'porch' visible on the left and we can see the station master's garden over the hedge. Bramber was an important port in the Middle Ages and the lower part of the mound with the remains of the castle and the ancient village church can just be seen rising behind. This section of line has now totally disappeared under the Bramber and Steyning bypass which follows it exactly at this point.

Opposite lower - Another ex LMS design Class 2 locomotive enters Bramber from the north on its way to Brighton. It is about to pass under the bridge which carried the Steyning road across the line, now replaced by a roundabout. Note the allotments alongside the line, a common feature in the 1960s. You can drive this route today!

Above - Not more than half a mile away was Steyning station, situated at the eastern end of this ancient and busy market town. Weekly markets for both live and dead stock were held here bringing in much traffic for the railway. Not only was there a thriving market in cattle from the surrounding agricultural area but sheep would be driven to Steyning from their pastures on the South Downs nearby. The station itself consisted of two platforms in a shallow cutting with beautifully kept flower beds as seen here in the summer of 1963. The agricultural nature of the area is in evidence in the huge storage barn behind the station.

The view from Steyning station approach looking towards Horsham showing the magnificent goods shed with its external hoisting crane to serve the upper storage floors. Also visible is the water crane at the end of the up platform. All the signals are 'off' probably indicating that the signal box has been switched out of use. The Steyning bypass now goes right through the site of the station platforms then diverges to the left at the point where the track in the picture bears right towards Henfield. The goods shed survives today converted into housing.

Opposite top - BR Standard Class 4 tank locomotive 80151, built at Brighton in January 1957 is seen here leaving Steyning in the summer of 1963 with a Horsham bound train formed of BR Mark 1 corridor stock. The goods yard has already closed and the weeds are taking over. The line is now dependent on its passenger traffic. Still the train service has recently been recast to provide a 'regular interval service' rather than the rather haphazard train times of the fifties and increased receipts are encouraging. 80151 spent the majority of its short ten year life in the Brighton area before being withdrawn from Eastleigh in May 1967. From there it was fortunately sold to Woodham Bros. scrapyard in Barry where it lay idle for many years before being rescued and restored. It can now be seen at the Bluebell Railway, one of its haunts when new.

Opposite lower - LMS design Class 2 No 41299, one of the batch which spent all their lives on the Southern, passes the up inner home signal as it enters Henfield. This afternoon train for Horsham is again formed of a Bulleid 3 coach set, the norm for this period. In the foreground is the 'ground signal', or 'dummy' as railwaymen called them, controlling the exit from the up siding. The trap points protect the mainline from runaway vehicles. The rust on the rails and the grass growing in the ballast indicate that the siding clearly hasn't been used for some time.

Above - A view from the same location but in the opposite direction showing another Class 2 locomotive leaving Henfield for Brighton, again with a Bulleid 3-coach set. The station platforms are visible beyond the train between it and the bridge over the road. At this period it was usual for locomotives to work with chimneys north i.e. facing Horsham. The entire station site has now disappeared under a housing development with only the name 'Beechings' and the 'Old Railway Tavern' to give any clue to its former existence. The irony is that Dr Beeching did not include this line in his closure proposals! The station at Henfield was quite close to the centre of the town and, with the significant housing development in the area, would have enjoyed substantial traffic had it been open today.

A BR Standard class 4 tank locomotive
approaches Henfield from the north and is
about to pass under the roadbridge and
enter the station. The train is formed of
Bulleid 3-coach set No 771. This was one
of a number of similar sets built by the
Birmingham Carriage and Wagon
Company for the Southern Railway
immediately prior to nationalisation in 1948.
This section of the line is now part of the
'Downs Link' footpath.

Opposite top - A view across the station platforms at Henfield. A Class 2 locomotive enters the station with a Horsham train. The down 'starting' signal visible behind the train still retains its old LBSCR wooden post although the signal arm has been replaced by a modern upper quadrant.

Opposite lower - For some unaccountable reason I never took any photographs of the next station, Partridge Green. Here in Spring 1964 Class 2 41294 is seen approaching West Grinstead from the south with steam to spare and is about to pass under the A272 road. The engine had a small narrow chimney, one of a number of variations in existence at the time. West Grinstead station itself is pictured on page 7 and 28/29. Shortly after this picture was taken Diesel Electric Multiple Units took over the over services on the line.

Above - Southwater station with Class 2 locomotive 41301 leaving with a southbound train and passing the diminutive LBSCR signal box. Southwater has seen enormous residential development, due to its proximity to Horsham and Gatwick, which would have sustained this section of the line. That the line closed in early 1966 was due more to incompetence and lack of foresight than economics. The diesel units were a success. However a shortage of them and the unwillingness of Government to allow the railways to buy any more meant that the line had to close. The steam locomotives and coaches had or were being withdrawn so nothing remained to work the services. Token bus services were provided but they didn't meet real needs and soon withered away. Closure of this line represented a massive failure of planning and illustrates the danger of focusing solely on short term gains. Electrification would not only have secured a desperately needed alternative route from London to Brighton but would also have satisfied huge potential traffic growth for Gatwick and London. Of course I'm glad my home town of Steyning is not swamped by commuters but the thought of a five minute walk to the local station rather than joining the hoards clogging local roads is very attractive!

Pages 28/29 - An Ivatt Class 2 locomotive hauls Bulleid 3 coach set 93 into West Grinstead station. The goods yard is closed, the signal box out of use. There were a number of different styles of signal box on the line but this must surely rank as the prettiest.

A last look at the rural tranquillity of the Steyning line. Class 2 locomotive 41326 nears Southwater bound for Horsham.

CHAPTER 3

The Hayling Island Line

The Southern had a handful of branch lines that were truly iconic and the line to Hayling Island must surely rank as one of these. For as long as anyone could remember the line had been operated using the ancient ex LBSCR A1X (Terrier) Class of locomotive, so called because of the power packed into a relatively small size and the distinctive 'bark' from their tall copper capped chimneys. These engines, now over eighty years old, performed valiantly with the often quite heavy trains. If the locomotives were predictable the rolling stock was not, the line being the repository of all sorts of quirky items over the years, as recent pictures in 'Southern Way' will testify. The single track branch left the junction of the ex LBSCR Brighton to Portsmouth and the ex LSWR Portsmouth Direct lines at Havant and followed a southward course for 4½ miles to its terminus at Hayling Island. Neither of the two intermediate stations, Langston or North Hayling, had goods yards or passing loops. Whereas most South Coast seaside resorts had shingle Hayling Island had a fine sandy beach and was therefore very popular with holidaymakers and day trippers. It was also easily accessible by train from London and the western suburbs.

Above - *A1X 32650* waits at Havant in the branch bay platform, situated at the eastern end of the down main platform, with a morning train for Hayling Island. The driver, boots polished and cap badge gleaming in the weak autumn sunlight, is rubbing his hands on his 'wiper' as he talks to his young fireman. In the siding behind the run round loop is a spare set of coaches including S1000S the experimental 'plastic coach'. The engine smokebox is showing burn marks, evidence of hard work.

Opposite top - After leaving Havant the line curved sharply away to the right over a level crossing before entering a wide cutting leading to a bridge where the line passed under the old A27 road. Here we see *A1X 32646* approaching the A27 bridge. The front of the engine has unfortunately been daubed with white paint which was the fashion with some crews at this time. The train is a summer weekend one with two BR Mark 1 compartment coaches plus a 2-coach Maunsell push pull set and a van for luggage and prams. This little train has seats for nearly 350 people, a testimony to how busy the branch was on summer weekends, when 12 coach electrics from Waterloo would disgorge a large proportion of their passengers at Havant to complete their journey on the 'Hayling Billy'.

Above - 32650 emerges from the south side of the A27 bridge. The engine, in common with all those working the line, carries a spark arrester at the top of the chimney to help prevent lineside fires. This addition however did not assist the engines' steaming capability.

At Langston crossing 32670 waits in the station with an up train, a van for luggage and prams at the front. The signalman stands ready to return the signals to danger and open the crossing gates after the train has left. The open air position would be pleasant enough in the summer but not much fun on a dark winter's evening. If it's a weekday he may get time to tend the cabbages and other vegetables in his flourishing allotment. If it's weekend he will be far too busy with a train every 15 minutes. 32670 as LBSCR No. 70 was sold to the independent Kent and East Sussex Railway in 1901 becoming their No 3 'Bodiam'. Upon nationalisation in 1948 it rejoined its classmates on the Southern system. Fortunately it now resides back at its KESR home.

32650 has stopped at Langston with an afternoon down train. The diminutive station, a short single platform with a waiting shelter and tiny ticket office, is hidden behind the coaches. This train consists of the Maunsell Brake Composite from push pull set 619 plus two ten compartment BR Mark 1 suburban coaches.

Langston Bridge, pictured here, had a severe axle load restriction and for this reason 'Terrier' locomotives had to be used on the line. They were the only engines capable of working the trains whilst being able to meet the weight limit. The adjacent road bridge also had a similar severe weight limit restricting the number of vehicles that could use it at any one time. This also limited the weight of the buses and even the number of passengers that they could carry. This favoured the railway which at peak times could and did, convey 700 passengers an hour each way together with their luggage. Unfortunately by the late 1950s both bridges needed replacement. The logical solution would have been to build a new combined road/rail bridge. However due to national and local government indifference to railways and a grant system which unfairly favoured road transport, a new road only bridge was built and the fate of the branch was thus sealed. It was yet another avoidable instance of traffic being forced onto the roads. I'm sure the holidaymakers would have preferred to cross the platform at Havant to a waiting train rather than be herded onto buses which couldn't cope with the influx.

Above - 32650 comes off Langston Bridge and on to the mainland with an up train formed this time of two ten compartment BR suburban coaches and a Maunsell Brake composite in between. The train is about to pass the fixed distant signal for Langston crossing. The locomotives on this line invariably worked with their chimney facing south.

Opposite top - A view from the shoreline of Langston Bridge with a maximum capacity up train. To allow for navigation, the bridge had a central opening span, controlled from the adjacent signal box. But this channel which had been dredged to form part of the Chichester – Portsmouth canal had fallen into disuse and the bridge had not been opened for years.

Opposite lower - 32670 nears the southern end of the bridge with a train for Hayling Island comprising four coaches and a van. The brand new road bridge mentioned previously can be seen in the background to the right of the train.

Opposite top - From the bridge the line ran along the shore almost all the way to Hayling Island. Photography from the west side was therefore difficult. At high tide the water came almost up to the track and at low tide a vast expanse of mud was exposed into which the unwary foot would quickly sink. This view taken from an up train window shortly after leaving Hayling Island shows the situation well.

Opposite lower - The second intermediate station was North Hayling. Although Langston had been rebuilt using standard SR concrete parts a few years before the line closed, North Hayling retained its simple wooden platform and rudimentary shelter. There appears to be no evidence of any lighting so this must have been a truly bleak place on a winter's evening in the teeth of a south westerly gale. The proximity to the shore is evident from the shingle. 32670 enters with a four coach train which will be much too long for the modest platform.

Above - North Hayling served a collection of houses, holiday homes, and bungalows strung out along the nearby road. Here 32650 moves off after setting down a couple of passengers. To save precious time, only one of the two trains which ran each hour on summer weekends stopped at North Hayling and Langston. The other one ran non stop between the termini and was allowed 10 minutes only as against 13 minutes for a 'stopper'.

Opposite top - 32650 is arriving at its destination, Hayling Island. There is a modest station building together with two platforms (main and bay), a run round loop, on which is situated a coaling platform, together with a goods yard and large goods shed. As it is a summer weekend a second train will be waiting in the bay platform to depart for Havant two minutes after this train has arrived. 32650 will uncouple then draw forward and run round its train. It will then draw the train out onto the single line and propel it into the bay platform to await the arrival of the next train. At Havant there was only one platform so an engine was always waiting in the loop ready to draw forward and then back onto the front of the train so as to be ready for departure, a five minute turn round time only being allowed. The arriving engine would uncouple and draw up to the buffer stops to take water, the only place on the line where this was possible. It would then wait in the loop once the train had departed. There were 25 trains each way on summer Saturdays in 1963, the last year of operation, and 21 each way on Sundays. Hardly a quiet uneconomic branch line!

Opposite lower - The fireman of 32646 hands the single line train staff to the signalman as the train enters the main platform at Hayling Island. The fireman of the train waiting in the bay platform behind us and to our left stands waiting to receive the train staff once the signalman has put it through the token instrument in the tiny signal box and obtained 'line clear' for the up train. The signalman's motor cycle XRV 154 is a 150 cc James Cadet.

Above - It wasn't always sunny at Hayling Island. Here 32646 waits with a two coach midweek train on a wet day. A passenger is in conversation with the driver whilst his family look on. I wonder whether the children remember this journey?

At the north end of Hayling Island station there had been, until a couple of years previously, two ex LBSCR starting signals. By 1963 only the one for the bay platform survived, the other had been replaced by a more modern signal. The building on the left is a small staff mess room complete with bowl on a stand outside for washing. The roses growing outside are evidence of the care railwaymen took of their working environment however humble. The piles of clinker next to the track show that fire cleaning has frequently taken place here before departure to ensure the engine will steam well on the journey to Havant.

Hayling Island line had yet one more peculiarity in store. It was one of the very few lines still to operate a mixed train, that is one conveying both passengers and freight. This left Hayling Island every weekday at 2.58 in the afternoon and is seen here on the approach to Langston Bridge. The working of the train was quite interesting. The engine with its passenger coaches would depart from the main platform at Hayling Island as normal, then stop and reverse into the neck of the goods yard to collect the wagons it had left there previously. When the guards of both the passenger and goods sections were ready it would set off again for Havant where it would arrive in the down main platform rather than the bay. A locomotive would come across from the up yard to collect the wagons after which the branch train would reverse back onto the branch line and draw forward into the bay to resume the normal service. There was also a down mixed train at 9.12 in the morning.

Without a new bridge the line was doomed and it closed on 3rd November 1963 the 'Terriers' being sent to Eastleigh for withdrawal. It was not only the residents of Hayling Island that were poorer as a result.

CHAPTER 4

The Isle of Wight

Of the truly iconic lines on the Isle of Wight just one, the Ryde to Ventnor line, features here. As a small child I can remember sitting on the beach at Ryde and seeing the little ex LSWR class O2 tank engines streaming up and down the Pier, their lengthy trains packed with holidaymakers. The certainty of seeing these old but beautifully maintained trains, the attractive hilly landscape and the seemingly endless sunshine made the Island a very special place.

Main view - The classic first view of the Island from the Portsmouth boat with the railway on the pier in the foreground and the church spire dominating the town of Ryde in the distance.

Inset - W35 'Freshwater' pulls out of Platform 3 at Ryde Pier Head station with its train. The platforms were just long enough to accommodate a six coach train with an engine each end. There was not room for engines to 'run round', an engine released by a previous departure or a light engine sent up from the depot at St. John's Road would couple to the front of the train to form the next departure. The Pier Tramway which conveyed passengers the length of the pier is in the foreground.

Overleaf - W18 'Ningwood' approaches Ryde Esplanade station which extended partly over the sea. The 6 coach Ventnor line train appears to comprise all ex LBSCR stock with the exception of the ex SECR brake coach at the rear. After the closure of the Sandown to Newport line in 1956 considerable standardisation was effected in regard to the operation of locomotives and trains. From then on all the engines faced south, to facilitate working the stiff climb from Shanklin to Ventnor and all the ex LBSCR brake vehicles were arranged brake end south at the south end of trains. The ex SECR brake vans, which had a much larger luggage capacity, were used at the north ends to minimise the movement of luggage at the cramped Pier Head station.

Opposite top - W33 'Bembridge' heads a Cowes line train between Ryde Esplanade and St. John's Road. Cowes trains usually comprised four coaches, the first vehicle here being an ex LBSCR brake followed by three ex SECR coaches. Between 1870 and 1881 the Pier Tramway continued along the esplanade and through the town to St. John's Road. It ran along this section of track-bed having joined it where the stream bears right in the middle distance. It closed when the railway opened in 1882.

Opposite lower - W17 'Seaview' runs into the down main platform at St. John's Road. The locomotive depot was behind the up platform to the left and the locomotive and carriage works where all the repairs and overhauls were done is to the right. The down loop platform saw little use. Trains on the Island used the LBSCR air brake system in contrast to the Mainland where the vacuum brake was standard. To power the brake the engines were fitted with a Westinghouse air pump situated on the left hand side of the smokebox and an air reservoir on top of the left hand tank, both clearly visible here.

Above - Ryde St. John's Road Works with W31 'Chale' under the hoist in June 1964. Unusually this engine carries a replacement 'Drummond' type boiler identifiable by the safety valves located in the top of the dome rather than in a separate casing in front of the cab. Front end lifting assistance appears to be available from an ancient crane 425S. This gem was built by Kirkstall Forge in 1865 and is seen here in its 99th year. It survived until 1966 and was surely the oldest item of standard gauge rolling stock in use in the British Isles. Much of the maintenance, painting and repair work was carried out during the winter with staff being redeployed on operational duties during the summer. Locomotives and coaches were always impeccably turned out and maintained in tip top condition. It was only in the final months of operation that standards began to slide.

Opposite top - W33 'Bembridge' is seen here north of Smallbrook Junction in June 1964 with a Cowes to Ryde train formed of three ex SECR coaches and an ex LBSCR brake at the far end. This section of track operated as a double line during the summer months with Smallbrook Junction signal box open to control the junction of the Cowes and Ventnor lines. In the winter however they were operated as two single lines with the junction at St. Johns Road. This accounts for the two 'haystack like' fog signalman's shelters situated either side of the tracks. The Ryde St. John's distant signals, for which the detonators fixed to the rails in times of fog would apply, were on the south side of the bridge from which this picture was taken. It must have been pretty uncomfortable sitting in these little huts but fog dense enough for them to be needed must have been rare. By the following summer they had disappeared.

Opposite lower - W22 'Brading', also carrying a Drummond boiler, is signalled onto the Ventnor line at Smallbrook Junction in the summer of 1964. It must be around 2 o'clock as the off duty signalman can be seen trudging along the track-bed to collect his motorcycle parked at the end of the access path a little further on but out of view. The locomotive is carrying a rectangular board indicating that it is performing loco duty 12. These boards were used on summer Saturdays to help busy signalmen identify locomotives and trains correctly.

Above - Earlier the same afternoon W24 'Calbourne' brings a Cowes line train past Smallbrook Junction as the signalman prepares to accept the single line token from the engine crew. W24 had received a full overhaul at Eastleigh Works the previous winter and had been returned to traffic in unlined black instead of the usual lined mixed traffic livery, probably as an economy measure. The brass nameplates were also replaced with painted ones at the same time, an omen of the rundown to come.

It's a summer Saturday afternoon and there has been a minor derailment at Ryde Pier Head, the worst time and place for such a thing to happen. Trains are starting to stack up in all directions. At such times lines were full to capacity and any problem, however small, meant delays. Here W18 'Ningwood' waits at Smallbrook Junction blocking the single line to Brading. The signalman is explaining the situation to the guard who will have to record the delay in his journal. The driver reads his paper, the fireman will be worrying about his fire.

57

Above - W17 'Seaview' leaves Brading with a train for Ryde in the summer of 1964. The train formation is a little unusual in that there are two ex LBSCR brake coaches at the rear. The only ex SECR vehicle in the formation appears to be the 'regulation' leading vehicle. The branch to Bembridge which left the Ventnor line at Brading closed in September 1953. Its course can be seen by the line of low bushes running across the picture just above the coaches.

Opposite top - Summer Saturdays were busy times for the signalman at Brading, so busy in fact that he had to have a 'runner' seen here waiting to collect the single line token from W27 'Merstone' as it enters the station with a down train. W20 'Shanklin' is already blowing off steam furiously, waiting for permission to enter the single line to Smallbrook. The track-bed of the former Bembridge branch can be seen on the right.

Opposite lower - W29 'Alverstone' is running into the down platform at Brading. The remote location of the signal box on the far right relative to the 'action' can be clearly seen. Operating this box on a summer Saturday must have been strenuous for both the signalman and his 'runner'. The four trains each way every hour on the single line to Smallbrook required the runner to collect the single line token from the crew, walk halfway down the platform, across the site of the former three tracks for the Bembridge branch, up the signalbox steps and give the token to the signalman. After giving 'train out of section' to Smallbrook and clearing the token through the instrument he would ask 'Is line clear?' for the up train. When the train is accepted he clears his points pulls off his signals and gets another token from the instrument. This the 'runner' would convey to the waiting up train. It was a good job that the section south to Sandown was double track, although trains would still have to be 'offered on', 'accepted' and signalled. I'm sure they were thankful that they didn't have to deal with the Bembridge branch trains as well!

Above - W17 'Seaview' enters Sandown with a southbound train. A northbound train can be seen disappearing in the distance. This will cross with the next southbound train at Brading. Although the locomotives were numbered into a separate series with a W prefix this W was not painted on the locomotives, there being no possibility of confusion with the mainland series of numbers except on paper!

Opposite top - Sandown station looking north with the signal box which curiously projected through the canopy on this the 'up' platform. To the left is the platform face for the line to Newport, closed in February 1956, and now used only as a siding. The Newport line track remained in situ for a hundred yards or so and was used to store some of the Island's antiquated goods stock, much of which hadn't turned a wheel in years. Whereas on the mainland such items would have been sent for scrap long ago here they were just left to rusticate quietly out of the way. The platforms appear deserted in this early summer 1964 view but would still frequently be absolutely packed with holidaymakers either arriving or departing.

Opposite lower - Late summer and W20 'Shanklin' is showing evidence of hard work as it leaves Sandown for Shanklin. The bracket signal would formerly have had an additional signal on the left hand side controlling entry to the Newport line platform. Between Sandown and Shanklin the line offered splendid views over the countryside and the sea.

Pages 62 and 63 - The line from Shanklin to Ventnor closed in April 1966 so for the last summer of steam operation trains terminated at Shanklin. A train has just arrived in the down platform. The 'shunt ahead' signal arm has been raised allowing the engine to shunt forward to run round its train, which will then be propelled forward and drawn back into the up platform ready for departure. The narrow road under-bridge looks as if it has had a few close encounters with over large vehicles.

Opposite top - Some of the most attractive countryside lay between Sandown and Ventnor as the line climbed towards the summit near the terminus. Here W30 'Shorewell' heads south in perfect weather with the customary ex LBSCR brake vehicle leading the train.

Opposite centre - Stooking corn by hand. How lucky I was to witness this scene and to be able to record it! I vaguely remember sights like this from the early 1950s but to see and photograph such an event in 1965 was unbelievable. Here we have an ancient tractor and reaper-binder working right next to the Ventnor line. Perhaps it was the difficulty and cost of transporting large combine harvesters to the Island which allowed the old ways to continue so long. Needless to say I have never seen this again.

Opposite lower - W33 'Bembridge' drifts into Wroxall station with a Ventnor train. The fireman is still adding coal to the fire as shown by the black smoke. Apse bank is behind him but there is still another mile to climb to the summit at Ventnor Tunnel. He will have a few minutes in the platform to raise some more steam while they wait for the train from Ventnor to cross.

Above - An overall view of Ventnor station perched high above the town, a gruelling walk for returning holidaymakers with their cases and bags. The yard is deserted apart from the odd wagon and van resting among the weeds. The 'caves' in the cliff were used by coal merchants.

Overleaf - W27 'Merstone' moves back onto its train after running round at Ventnor. The tunnel started immediately at the north end of the station and crews would have to be alert to give the signalman the single line token as soon as they came out of the tunnel. In front of the engine is an inspection pit to enable the driver to top up the oil in the engine's inside motion if required. The platform arrangement was curious with the main platform line having faces on both sides as can be seen. On the further side, and controlled by the left hand signal, is the second face of the island platform. There was however no means of getting access to this platform except by a narrow gangplank which would be thrown across the near line when required. Not surprisingly this platform saw little use although I do remember as a child being on a school excursion train which departed from there. The line between Shanklin and this station closed in April 1966, the line to Cowes had succumbed in the February of the same year. The section from Shanklin to Ryde was electrified during the winter of 1966/7 with the service resuming using old ex London Transport tube trains. The problem with the Island's railways has always been the very narrow tunnel between Esplanade and St John's Road which prevented more modern locomotives and coaches being used and ensured the line was always in a 'time warp' The line is still open, just. But it was in a very run down condition when I saw it last! One can only hope that some day someone will realise the potential and give it back some of the pride it once had.

CHAPTER 5

The Lewes to East Grinstead Line,

The Lewes and East Grinstead line was an unlikely candidate for a battle over line closures, as mentioned earlier. In fact this particular line deserved to close. Unlike its counterparts, the Steyning line and the Eastbourne to Tunbridge Wells line, which served many towns and villages, the Lewes and East Grinstead line ran through vast tracts of open countryside. Indeed it seemed to deliberately avoid any towns and villages it might have served apart from Barcombe and Sharpthorn with its station at West Hoathly. All the other stations were, and still are, far from any habitation. This was in part intentional: the stations were to be railheads for goods traffic rather than convenient stops for passengers. This may have been fine in its heyday but when by the early 1950s goods traffic had all but vanished the line had nothing left to sustain it. A mere quirk of fate dictated that part of such a non viable line, namely the section from Sheffield Park to Horsted Keynes, should, in 1959, have been the nucleus of the first of the standard gauge railway preservation schemes, the Bluebell Railway. Now very much a going concern.

Right - All the station buildings on the line followed the same general 'Country House' design. Newick and Chailey is seen here from the approach road as it was in September 1964, after closure. This station was an unusual variant on the design with two storeys on the road side and three on the platform side, necessitated by its location in a cutting. Walking through the Booking Hall one would arrive at the top of the footbridge linking the two platforms. The up side platform and footbridge were demolished in the early 1930s with only the steps to the down platform remaining.

Ardingly Branch & early Bluebell

Opposite top - Ex SECR P class locomotive No 27 (BR No 31027) stands in the up platform at Sheffield Park in October 1963 resplendent in full SECR livery. Sadly it is no longer in this condition and has lain dismantled for years awaiting restoration. Perhaps one day….

Opposite lower - Ex North London Railway tank locomotive 2650 (BR no. 58850) waits to leave Sheffield Park with a summer weekday train in 1965. The train consists of the ex London and North Western Railway Observation coach and an ex SECR 'Birdcage' brake. This locomotive, designed primarily for shunting and goods work, produced a lively ride for both crew and passengers at 25 mph but was powerful and economical in use.

Above - The exterior of Sheffield Park station seen in October 1964. The similarity to Newick and Chailey is clear. My Fordson 5-cwt van parked outside completes the scene. How I wish I still had it today!

Horsted Keynes station with a two coach electric train ready to depart for Ardingly and Haywards Heath. This was the only electrified platform and yet had no canopy: it had been removed in the 1930s. The Southern Railway had plans to electrify the line through to East Grinstead and East Croydon, thus creating an alternative route to Brighton, but World War 2 intervened and Horsted Keynes was as far as the scheme got. The electric train is interesting in that it is 2 BIL unit 2056 but running with a HAL trailer (nearest the camera). This unique combination doubtless resulted from the fact that its original trailer must have been damaged beyond repair at some time. The picture was taken in October 1963 when the service had only a few more days to run. The line to Haywards Heath was to close on the 28th of that month.

Opposite top - Before the line closed however a couple of specials were run. The first in September 1963 featured the preserved Caledonian Railway single wheeler No 123 seen here at Horsted Keynes and preserved T9 No 120. The coal has been specially whitewashed for the event. On the footplate the locomotive inspector in his bowler hat is keeping a watchful eye on proceedings.

Opposite lower - The second of these pre closure specials ran on the last day of the branch's operation. 'Stepney' and 'Birch Grove', two Bluebell locomotives, are pictured here at Ardingly pulling the set of coaches which formed the 'Lancing Belle' en route to Sheffield Park from Brighton. The jostling crowds, sometimes displaying insufficient regard for safety, who are drawn to last day specials are admittedly not to everyone's taste.

Right - The branch to Ardingly closed and demolition began. The contractors soon found that their diminutive diesel engine was totally inadequate for hauling wagons on the line's 1 in 75 gradients, so they hired a Bluebell engine and crew to do the work. Here North London tank 2650 rests atop Lywood Viaduct just to the west of Horsted Keynes. Although the viaduct has since been demolished the location is still readily visible from the Z bend in the road.

Opposite top - West Hoathly, the first station on the double track section of line north of Horsted Keynes, was very similar to Sheffield Park. In this view we see the entrance and the station master's house which were on the up (west) side of the line. This picture was taken during the line's demolition and a redundant signal arm resides in the porch. One of the contractor's vehicles, which was probably being used for dragging rails or sleepers along the track, can be seen on the left. Outside the station master's house is a Panther Model 100 motorcycle.

Opposite lower - West Hoathly signal box is seen here shortly before its demolition at the East Grinstead end of the down platform. As the line was double track throughout there were no single line tokens to exchange and the signal box was located here to provide a good view of the yard and the down siding. The current signal box at Kingscote, which occupies a similar position, is a reconstruction of the one formerly at Brighton Upper Goods. This has been installed in preparation for the final phase of extension of the present line from Sheffield Park to East Grinstead.

This page top - A view from the down platform looking north towards East Grinstead. The covered footbridge really is quite exquisite. Sheffield Park and Newick and Chailey originally had similar structures but they were removed in the Southern Railway's 1930 economy drive leaving this the only survivor. At this time the Bluebell Railway was preoccupied with securing the future of the line between Sheffield Park and Horsted Keynes and had no thoughts of extending northwards. This fine structure was pulled down shortly after this picture was taken and the station buildings subsequently demolished.

This page lower - Ex LBSCR Class E4 473 'Birch Grove' rests at West Hoathly station between duties on the demolition trains. The North London tank engine 2650 was the preferred candidate for this duty with 473 deputising when 2650 needed a washout or maintenance.

Opposite top - Kingscote station in September 1964 and the weeds are beginning to take over. Note the wartime striping on the canopy columns. Remarkably this was still visible when the Bluebell Railway purchased the station some 20 years later. This station was not reopened in 1958 when British Railways was forced to restart the line's train service as it was not mentioned in the original Act of Parliament. Fortunately the station building, canopy, and the upside platform survived virtually intact although the latter had completely disappeared beneath undergrowth when the Bluebell took over, The downside platform and canopy had been demolished however and has had to be rebuilt. This station had a subway connecting the platforms and this too survived even down to the handrails and light fittings although completely filled with rubble.

Opposite lower - Bluebell Railway North London Tank 2650 heads through Horsted House Farm over-bridge north of Horsted Keynes with a demolition train in September 1964. The section of line from Horsted Keynes to Kingscote has now been reopened but with single rather than double track. The soot marks on the left hand (up) side of the bridge have been caused by numerous locomotives over the years toiling against the 1 in 75 gradient here.

Above - This time 2650 is just south of Imberhorne Viaduct with a bogie bolster heading off to collect another load of rails.

Next page - Journey's end, well nearly…A trail of steam floats above North London Tank 2650 as it crosses Imberhorne Viaduct at East Grinstead. The train itself is totally dwarfed by this massive structure. It has just dropped off its load of rails and other materials at the lower yard at East Grinstead and is returning with its wagons empty.

Demolition was completed in early 1965 after which 2650 returned to Sheffield Park by low loader. In 1971 after purchasing the line between Sheffield Park and Horsted Keynes the Bluebell Railway announced its intention of pushing north to East Grinstead. This has been a protracted undertaking which hopefully will reach fruition in the near future.

CHAPTER 6

The 'Cuckoo' Line

The rural connotations of a name taken from Mayfield's annual 'Cuckoo Fair', belie the true nature of a line which linked the major urban centres of Eastbourne and Tunbridge Wells and which passed through sizeable towns like Hailsham and Heathfield. Diverging from the main Eastbourne to Lewes line at Polegate it ran north to join the line from Uckfield to London line just west of Eridge.

Above - Hailsham station, the first on the line, located in the centre of quite a large town, features in this view from the road bridge. In the up platform three coach 'East Sussex' Diesel Electric Multiple Unit 1304 waits with a train to Tunbridge Wells. Whereas most trains ran through from Eastbourne to Tunbridge Wells West they were supplemented with shuttles on the Eastbourne to Hailsham section. The neat little ex LBSCR Signal Box is located on the platform itself.

Opposite top - The next stop was Hellingly. Subtle variations to the familiar 'Country House' station design include in this instance an external canopy and enlarged booking office. The station served a small village only until a massive asylum was built in the neighbourhood. For this a mile and a quarter long branch line was constructed.

Opposite lower - Hellingly station again, this time from the platform side. A three coach DEMU is heading towards Eastbourne. By now, in September 1964, all trace of the Asylum railway has disappeared. All that can be seen is an open grassy space where once adjacent to the track had been its platform. The railway in question had been acquired and electrified by the County Council when the asylum opened in 1903. In 1932 the platform was removed. Coal to feed the asylum boilers continued to be hauled up the line by an antique electric locomotive until 1959. The 'Cuckoo' line was single track throughout but all the stations had passing loops except for Hellingly.

The next station, at Horam, looking north. DEMU 1310 can be seen waiting in the down platform as the driver receives the single line train staff from the signalman. As there was no footbridge to connect the platforms passengers were expected to use the road bridge.

Opposite top - Horam, seen here from the approach road looking east.

Opposite lower - The line could be very busy as seen here at Horam on a September afternoon in 1964. A three coach DEMU heads for Eastbourne with a six coach train, formed of two three coach units, heading in the opposite direction for Tunbridge Wells. The signal box is tucked under the canopy. The signalman can be seen under the canopy walking along to collect the single line train staff. He could probably attend to other station duties also given the relocation of the signal box by the Southern Railway in the 1930s. Another noteworthy feature here is the unusual separately roofed building which has been added on the canopy on the left hand platform. Although the goods yard may well have been closed by this time it appears nonetheless to hold plentiful supplies for the local coal merchant.

Above - The principal station on the line was Heathfield, pictured here in September 1964. This photograph was taken from the road bridge and shows the station building that was set at right angles to the platforms on the road above. It was situated close to the town centre and was busy enough to warrant a W H Smith bookstall.

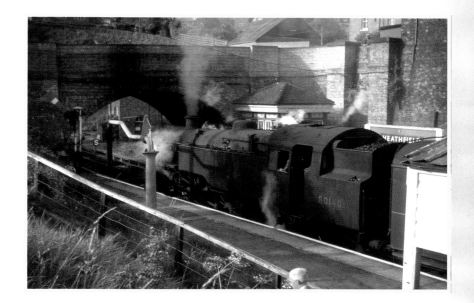

Main picture - This general view of Heathfield station and goods yard gives a good idea of vastness of the site. To the right of the 3 coach DMU bound for Eastbourne, the coal yard can be seen still doing good business. This site is now totally converted to housing

Insert left - The station building at Heathfield can be seen with the covered steps which passengers used as access to the 'down' platform. Passengers for up trains were expected to cross the road bridge and use a path down to the platform. A neat little LBSCR signalbox stands at the end of the platform by the bridge. The gas storage facility for Heathfield station's natural gas lighting was located between this bridge and Heathfield Tunnel beyond it.

Insert right - Although DEMUs worked most trains at this time some workings were still steam hauled. Here BR standard class 4 locomotive 80140 is about to depart from Heathfield with an up train. The base of the water tank building which supplied the water cranes at the end of each platform can be seen through the bridge. The water crane in the foreground has a bent arm whereas the original LBSCR one was straight. This adaptation was introduced primarily to make it easier for 'West Country' class locomotives to take water but were a boon for any modern locomotive with a their high water fillers. A passenger can be seen in the foreground on the path up to the road.

Early April 1965 and the DMUs have gone, sent elsewhere to make up for shortages, an ominous sign for the future of this line. BR Standard class 4 tank 80152 seen waiting here at Heathfield with a couple of odd BR Standard Mark 1 coaches was one of the last three completed at Brighton Works in February 1957. It ran until July 1967 when the era of steam came to an end on the Southern. At this point it had only been in service for 10 years and for much of the time engaged in light work like this. Given normal repair and maintenance, engines such as these would easily have served another 20 years.

Opposite top - Mayfield station looking across from the up to the down platform. This station like several others on this line has a platform signal box and a substantial canopy. A subway, just visible beyond the signal box links the platforms.

Opposite lower - Mayfield again, seen this time from the opposite direction has the signal box and subway clearly visible in the foreground.

This page top - The station building at Mayfield photographed from the approach road. It has a much longer station building than many because of its considerably enlarged facilities although its basic design is the same.

This page lower - A 3 coach DEMU on the line north of Mayfield.

Above - Rotherfield and Mark Cross, the next station on the line, seen here in September 1964 with Standard class 4 tank 80149 on a four coach Eastbourne train formed of coaches of the narrow Maunsell Restriction 1 type. It is fair to assume that this particular train began its journey at Tonbridge hence the use of Restriction 1 coaches rather than the more usual Restriction 4 coaches because the latter were not allowed on the Tonbridge to Tunbridge Wells West section. The Restriction 1 coaches pictured here were amongst the last remaining Maunsell vehicles to survive. The LBSCR water crane has the original straight arm fitted and behind this can be seen a concrete Southern railway 'lamp room'. Both running lines have been re-laid with concrete sleepers but retain bullhead rail.

Opposite top - It is late May 1965 and a filthy BR Standard Class 4 tank 80032 stops at Rotherfield and Mark Cross with a three coach Bulleid set heading for Tunbridge Wells. It's no wonder the engine looks neglected, the closure notices have been posted and the trains will stop running on 14th June. No one cares any more.

Opposite lower - The same train looking towards Tunbridge Wells. At least there has been some attempt to clean the engine number and the BR crest. The spring grass is starting to grow through the platform surface and the rails in the goods yard beyond the platforms have been lifted. The three and six coach stop boards for the DEMU service can be seen on the left. This station has electric lights on the platform with characteristic SR concrete lamp posts and shades.

Here at Tunbridge Wells West where the 'Cuckoo' line trains usually terminated, 80084 waits in the loop with an Eastbourne train. The train crew have a chat, perhaps about the impending closure or maybe about football! 80084 has just come off shed with its bunker full of good coal. This locomotive was to be withdrawn from service on 13th June in just a few days time when the line closed. Tunbridge Wells West had once been a thriving hub on the old LBSCR network with its busy engine shed and carriage sidings and an extremely well patronised commuter service. The frequent late arrival of trains to and from the capital in the early 1950s did not amuse 'Disgruntled of Tunbridge Wells' and he was not afraid of saying so. As a result the shed received an allocation of these Standard class 4 tanks when new. However things were already going downhill with the withdrawal of the trains to Eastbourne. Remaining services, including the commuter trains, were in 1971 reduced to a mere shuttle between Eridge and Tonbridge. Complete closure came in 1985. So what is the site used for today? A Supermarket and a Car Park!

A further volume of unpublished colour material from Terry Cole again featuring the Southern Region in the Sixties, is in the early stages of preparation.